CENGAGE Learning

Literary Newsmakers for Students, Volume 1

Project Editor
Anne Marie Hacht **Editorial**
Sara Constantakis and Ira Mark Milne **Rights Acquisition and Management**
Margaret Chamberlain-Gaston and Sue Rudolph **Manufacturing**
Drew Kalasky

Imaging
Lezlie Light, Mike Logusz, and Kelly Quin **Product Design**
Pamela A. E. Galbreath **Vendor Administration**
Civie Green **Product Manager**
Meggin Condino © 2006 Gale, a part of Cengage Learning Inc.

For more information, contact
Gale, an imprint of Cengage Learning

errors, omissions or discrepancies. Gale, an imprint of Cengage Learning accepts no payment for listing; and inclusion in the publication of any organization, agency, institution, publication, service, or individual does not imply endorsement of the editors or publisher. Errors brought to the attention of the publisher and verified to the satisfaction of the publisher will be corrected in future editions.

ISBN 1414402813
ISSN 1559-9639

Printed in the United States of America

10 9 8 7 6 5 4 3 2 1

Will in the World: How Shakespeare Became Shakespeare

Stephen Greenblatt 2004

Introduction

Stephen Greenblatt's *Will in the World: How Shakespeare Became Shakespeare* (2004) is a biography of William Shakespeare. In it, Greenblatt proposes to answer the question of how a man with only a secondary school education, the son of a small town glove maker, became the most renowned playwright of all time. As with other persons in Elizabethan England—England during the reign of Queen Elizabeth I, 1558–1603—there are records of Shakespeare's life. Some of these correspond to the usual signposts: birth, marriage, and death. Scattered records of other moments, especially of transactions in which he was involved, also exist. In all, however, they form only a sketchy trail with considerable gaps. Greenblatt builds entire scenarios around the limited evidence. He connects what is known about key moments in Shakespeare's life to what historians have learned about what was going on at those moments in England. He then relates both the personal history and the larger social history to Shakespeare's plays and poetry.

Will in the World is only one of several books by major scholars of Shakespeare to come out at around the same time. These books, the fruits of a generation of scholarship, sum up insights and appreciation that have developed over decades of teaching and research. Some, like *Shakespeare* (2002), by David Bevington, and *The Age of Shakespeare* (2004), by Frank Kermode, are similar to *Will in the World* in that they draw connections between Shakespeare's art and his life and times. But no scholar has been more influential in promoting this approach to the study of literature in general and Shakespeare in particular than Greenblatt. His *Will in the World* has attracted more readers than any other contemporary book on Shakespeare. It is therefore having a major impact on our understanding of Shakespeare today.

Author Biography

Stephen Greenblatt is widely recognized as a leading academic scholar and public intellectual. That is, he has risen to the top of academia, or the professional world of university teaching and research. He has also reached beyond academia to address his writings and lectures to less specialized audiences. In 2002, he was named John Cogan University Professor of the Humanities at Harvard University, one of the most prestigious faculty appointments at one of the world's leading universities.

Greenblatt was born on November 7, 1943, in Cambridge, Massachusetts. He is the son of Harry J. Greenblatt, a lawyer, and Mollie Greenblatt. As a youth, he attended Newtown High School, where a favorite English teacher, John Harris, helped to influence him in his choice of career. He went on to study at Yale University, from which he earned a bachelor's degree in 1964 and a doctorate in 1969, and at Cambridge University in England, from which he earned a master of philosophy degree in 1966. His principal mentor at Yale was Alvin Kernan, the author of *The Cankered Muse: Satire of the English Renaissance* (1959).

Greenblatt began his distinguished teaching career in the English Department of the University of California at Berkeley in 1969; he remained on the faculty there until 1997, when he moved to

Harvard. The National Endowment for the Humanities recognized him with their young humanist award in 1971–1972. At Berkeley, Greenblatt's work was influenced by the French philosopher Michel Foucault, who began teaching there in 1975. This influence was an important factor in Greenblatt's development of New Historicism.

New Historicism, sometimes known as Cultural Studies, is a practice of interpreting texts in their historical context, or in relation to the time and place in which they were written. It is also a set of theories about how texts are shaped by large social and historical forces—not simply the individual creativity of their authors. In "Pretending to Be Real: Stephen Greenblatt and the Legacy of Popular Existentialism," Paul Stevens writes that Greenblatt's first major New Historicist book, *Renaissance Self-Fashioning: From More to Shakespeare*, (1980), "marked a major change in the direction of English studies." Greenblatt went on to publish many other influential books on the literature and culture of the Renaissance, or early modern period. These include *Shakespearean Negotiations: The Circulation of Social Energy in Renaissance England* (1988), *Learning to Curse: Essays in Early Modern Culture* (1990), *Marvelous Possessions: The Wonder of the New World* (1991), and *Hamlet in Purgatory* (2001). He is also the editor of the Norton Shakespeare, and of several collections of essays by other scholars. All of these publications are published by academic presses, and they have been read mainly by university students and faculty. *Will in the World: How Shakespeare Became Shakespeare* (2004), is the first of his major books to be addressed to a broader audience of interested readers, both inside and outside of academia. It was nominated for numerous awards, including the National Book Critics Circle Award and the Pulitzer Prize.

As of 2005, Greenblatt is the John Cogan University Professor of the Humanities at Harvard University in Boston. He is married to Ramie Targoff and has three sons.

Chapter 1: Primal Scenes

Greenblatt borrows the title of the first chapter of *Will in the World: How Shakespeare Became Shakespeare* from psychiatrist Sigmund Freud. However, unlike the deeply intimate "primal scenes" of early childhood described in Freud's psychoanalytic theory, the scenes that Greenblatt considers are the very public spectacles that Shakespeare would have been exposed to in his rural hometown of Stratford-upon-Avon. As a student, Shakespeare would have read and participated in performances of Latin comedies. Perhaps, Greenblatt speculates, he starred in a performance of a play called *The Two Menaechmuses*, which became a source for Shakespeare's own *Comedy of Errors*. Traveling troupes of actors came through town, and Shakespeare might have attended their exciting performances in the company of his father, who served a term as bailiff, or mayor. They staged morality plays, which delivered lessons about vices and virtues through simple plots and characters that stood for abstract principles, such as Youth or Chaos. Shakespeare later emulated these works by writing for a broad audience, but he also improved upon them by making his characters resemble real people. His plays also show the influence of the folk festivals that he would have seen as a youth.

Greenblatt concludes the chapter with a description of the likely impact of a visit by Queen Elizabeth to the region; she stayed at the nearby castle of Earl of Leicester, who staged elaborate entertainments for her. Such "primal scenes" would have influenced Shakespeare's development as a playwright.

Chapter 2: The Dream of Restoration

Shakespeare grew up in a society in which occupations and lifestyles were tightly regulated. His father, John, was a glove maker who also drew income by illegally trading in wool and dealing in loans and property. John aspired not only for prosperity, but also for promotion in rank—to become a gentleman. Greenblatt deduces that during the time between the end of Shakespeare's formal schooling—around 1580—and his professional emergence in London in the 1590s, Shakespeare was involved in his father's work. The figurative language of his plays is rife with knowledgeable references to gloves and leather. The plays also refer frequently to drinking; Greenblatt speculates that alcoholism might have been a cause of a collapse of John's fortunes. After reaching a height of prosperity and status during Shakespeare's early adolescence, John fell into debt and lost his social standing. Greenblatt suggests that the family's hardships may be the reason for Shakespeare's artistic preoccupation with what Greenblatt calls "the dream of restoration": many of Shakespeare's characters, such as the exiled Prospero and Miranda of *The Tempest*, suffer such reversals, only to be restored to their proper station by the end of the play. Perhaps, the opportunity to act and dress like a gentleman was what attracted Shakespeare to the theatre in the first place. Greenblatt suggests that, as a successful playwright and businessman, Shakespeare was behind a successful application to have John recognized as a gentleman through the gaining of a family coat of arms—a status that Shakespeare would inherit.

Chapter 3: The Great Fear

The England of Shakespeare's youth had suffered through decades of vicious religious conflict between Catholics and Protestants under the Tudor dynasty. Upon her ascension to the throne in 1558, the Anglican Protestant Queen Elizabeth reversed the policies of her half-sister Mary (who had reigned from 1553) and made Protestantism the state religion—practicing Catholicism became a crime. The persecution of Catholics created a climate of fear that drove many people to carry on their religious practice in secret; they were Protestants in public but Catholics in private. Greenblatt suggests that Shakespeare's mother was probably a devoted Catholic and that his father might have played both roles. Shakespeare may have experienced a deeply conflicted household. Drawing on evidence that he acknowledges to be controversial, Greenblatt suggests that Shakespeare might have spent part of his young adulthood working as a schoolmaster for wealthy Catholic families in Lancashire, in the north of England, which was a stronghold of recusancy, or the refusal to accept Protestantism. There, Shakespeare may have gotten his start as an actor with regional troupes, but he would also have been exposed to the dangers associated with the secret practice of Catholicism. He may have met Edmund Campion, a notorious Catholic missionary who was publicly executed. Shakespeare's plays indicate a temperament that would not have been attracted to religious extremism, but they also show how such experiences captured his imagination.

Chapter 4: Wooing, Wedding and Repenting

In 1582, back in Stratford, eighteen-year-old Shakespeare married Anne Hathaway, who was eight years older, independent, and already pregnant with Shakespeare's first daughter, Susanna. He then spent most of his adult life living away from his family, in London. When he died in 1616, he left Anne out of his will, bequeathing her only, as an apparent afterthought, his "second best bed." These circumstances suggest that Will did not have a happy marriage. Greenblatt interprets Shakespeare's plays and poetry in light of this likelihood; his works show mixed feelings, at best, about marriage. The chapter title comes from words spoken by Beatrice, a heroine of *Much Ado About Nothing*. They suggest a pessimistic view in which couples meet, fall in love, marry, and fall out of love. Beatrice and her lover, Benedick, are perhaps the only couple in Shakespeare's principal comedies that actually seem to have a good prospect for the future; other couples seem ill-matched. In the plays considered as "problem comedies," such as *Measure for Measure*, characters are forced to marry against their will—as Greenblatt suspects was the case with Shakespeare. Perhaps this is why Shakespeare stresses the importance of avoiding premarital sex in plays like *Romeo and Juliet* and *The Tempest*. Those mature married couples in his plays who do maintain intimacy, such as Macbeth and Lady Macbeth, have disturbingly warped relationships. However, Shakespeare's sonnets show that he did experience love—but only outside of marriage.

Chapter 5: Crossing the Bridge

What brought Shakespeare, in the mid-1580s, to leave Anne and their three small children to go make his fortune in London? Greenblatt explores a story that emerged in the late seventeenth century that Shakespeare was seeking to escape punishment after having been caught illegally hunting, or poaching, for deer on the property of his powerful neighbor, Sir Thomas Lucy. He suggests that this story might have been a front for a more serious clash with Lucy, who was a devoted Protestant and a persecutor of secret Catholics. Lucy was involved in the arrests and investigations that led to the deaths of Shakespeare's distant relations, John Somerville and Edward Arden, both condemned as

Catholic traitors. It is possible that Shakespeare, too, had something to fear.

It is also possible that he had the opportunity to join up with a prestigious troupe of players, the Queen's Men, who were in Stratford in 1587 and possibly had an opening for a young actor. His arrival in London would have been exciting. It was a teeming city, dangerous, rapidly changing, with impressive architecture and sights. It would become the model for the urban settings in Shakespeare's plays. It is likely that Shakespeare's point of entry into the city was London Bridge, where he would have seen the heads of Somerville and Arden still on spikes. The fate of these relatives might give a clue to the lack of information now available for Shakespeare's biographers—in that dangerous political climate, Shakespeare learned to be secretive and private.

Chapter 6: Life in the Suburbs

Londoners looked outside city limits for entertainment, to the less regulated "liberties," or suburbs. Some of the suburban pastimes were violent and gory, such as the popular spectator sport of bull-or bear-baiting (the animals were tied to stakes and attacked by dogs). The suburbs were also home to whorehouses. Shakespeare assuredly also witnessed the severe physical punishments and executions of criminals that were a routine spectacle on London streets. That these sights drew Shakespeare's interest is evident in his plays.

Among the spectacles that he would have seen were the theaters themselves, which were just emerging during the late sixteenth century. Religious and civic authorities felt the theaters, like other entertainments, were immoral and dangerous, and they tried to close them down. To make enough money, theaters had to draw repeat customers with a large repertory of plays; thus, there was considerable demand for a productive playwright. Shakespeare was inspired by his contemporary Christopher Marlowe, who was the same age and of similar background. Marlowe's *Tamburlaine* would have been one of the first plays that Shakespeare saw in London.

Tamburlaine, with its exotic setting, its ambitious scope, its disregard for conventional morality, and its high poetic language, was utterly different from the plays he had seen in his youth. Shakespeare's first plays, especially the *Henry VI* trilogy, were clearly influenced by Marlowe. While Shakespeare lacked Marlowe's formal education and scholarly reading, his friend Richard Field, a printer, would have given him access to source material. Shakespeare's early history plays are inferior to his later work, but they were quite popular, and announced the arrival of a new major playwright.

Chapter 7: Shakescene

As he began to make his reputation in London, Shakespeare would have come in contact with the

University Wits, the social circle of poets who wrote for the stage. The members of this group came from a variety of class backgrounds, but they had in common their degrees from Cambridge or Oxford, a fondness for drink, and a tendency for reckless, even criminal behavior. The group included the brilliant Christopher Marlowe, and Robert Greene, whom Greenblatt describes as "larger than life, a hugely talented, learned, narcissistic, self-dramatizing, self-promoting, shameless, and undisciplined scoundrel." Perhaps, initially, the University Wits would have been intrigued by and appreciative of the author of the *Henry VI* trilogy, despite his provincial upbringing and grammar school education. But whether by their choice or his, he did not join the group and did not adopt their lifestyle. He was an outsider and a rival. As his career was soaring in the early 1590s, the University Wits were meeting premature deaths from disease, violence, and dissipation. In a posthumous book attributed to Greene, the author insulted Shakespeare, calling him "an upstart Crow, beautified with our feathers." Shakespeare responded by parodying their works in his own plays, and by creating his great comic character, Falstaff. Falstaff, the carousing, witty, "fat knight" featured in *Henry IV Part One, Henry IV Part Two, Henry V,* and the *Merry Wives of Windsor*, was unmistakably modeled after Robert Greene.

Chapter 8: Master-Mistress

This chapter focuses on the poetry that

Shakespeare wrote apart from his plays—especially his 154 sonnets. These were circulated in manuscript form well before they were printed as *Shakespeares Sonnets* in 1609. While the speaker of each sonnet ("I") is unambiguously Shakespeare, the addressee ("you") and other persons referred to are cunningly cloaked, so that scholars have been guessing at their identities for centuries. This effect was intentional. Shakespeare wrote the sonnets with the intention that only a very limited audience would understand them in their specific meanings. Greenblatt speculates that the first seventeen sonnets were commissioned for Henry Wriothesley, the Earl of Southhampton, a beautiful young aristocrat who was resisting considerable pressure to marry. These sonnets take the unconventional approach of encouraging the addressee to marry not out of love for a woman, but out of self-love: to replicate himself by having a child in his own image. In the process of making this argument, and in many of the 154 sonnets, the poet evinces his own love for this "master-mistress." Shakespeare explicitly dedicated his poems "Venus and Adonis" and "The Rape of Lucrece" to Southhampton. The highly sensual former poem, one of the few works Shakespeare purposively had printed, was a popular success. Greenblatt suggests that in seeking an aristocratic patron, Shakespeare might have been trying to offset his loss of income from the temporary closings of the theatres because of civil unrest and the bubonic plague.

Chapter 9: Laughter at the Scaffold

Shakespeare's comedy *The Merchant of Venice* was a response to his rival Christopher Marlowe's own play about a Jewish villain, *The Jew of Malta*. Even though Jews were the sources of Judeo-Christian tradition, the evil figure of the Jew filled a crucial "symbolic role" as the ultimate outsider: anti-Christian and even inhuman. Barabas in *The Jew of Malta*, with his boundless hatred of Christianity, fulfills this role precisely: he has no redeeming characteristics. In that play and in his other work, Marlowe seemed to speak to his audience's fear and hatred of foreigners. The Jews had long since been expelled from England, but xenophobic mobs, or people who are fearful of foreign people and places, periodically attacked existing communities of immigrants. Shakespeare, in his contribution to the composition of an unperformed play, *Sir Thomas More*, actually had More oppose such mob violence. More importantly, Shylock, the Jew in *The Merchant of Venice*, demanded the audience's sympathy even as he excited their hatred. Greenblatt attributes this difference from Marlowe to Shakespeare's reaction to the case of Rodrigo Lopez, a physician to the Queen who was accused of plotting to poison her. Lopez, a professed Christian, was of Jewish origin, and his accusers claimed he still adhered to Judaism. The spectators at his execution laughed when he insisted on his innocence and his faith. The audience may have laughed at Shylock as well, but they would have been discomfited by their recognition of his common humanity.

Chapter 10: Speaking with the Dead

By 1600, it would seem that no accomplishment was lacking from Shakespeare's career—yet he entered into a brilliant new phase with the creation of a masterpiece, *Hamlet*. Shakespeare's great innovation was his display of inwardness—the state of his characters' troubled minds. Through his earlier work, Shakespeare had been steadily improving on the form of the soliloquy, or the speeches in which characters, alone on the stage, speak their thoughts aloud. Shakespeare adapted an old story about the Danish prince that had been produced as a play before and was available in published sources. In the earlier versions, the prince feigns madness as a child in order to stall for time, so that he can grow up and avenge his father's death. Shakespeare's character Hamlet, already a young adult, pretends to be crazy for no clear reason. This uncertainty makes his psychological state the focus of the play. Greenblatt suggests that the tragedy's emotional power might derive from Shakespeare's reaction to the death of his son, Hamnet, in 1596 (his name echoes "Hamlet") and the impending death of his father, in the context of the religious conflicts discussed in Chapter 3. Protestants banned Catholic funeral practices such as paying for masses to speed the passage of the deceased through Purgatory, the holding area between Heaven and Hell where the dead suffer while atoning their sins. But for people who believed in Purgatory, such as, perhaps, Shakespeare's parents, and possibly the playwright himself, their inability to help their dead loved ones would have been anguishing.

Chapter 11: Bewitching the King

By omitting the rationale for Hamlet's feigned madness, Shakespeare created opacity: a lack of transparency, a dark uncertainty that engages the spectator or reader in a limitless exploration into the depths of character. In his subsequent great tragedies, *Othello* and *King Lear*, Shakespeare similarly adapted his sources through the process Greenblatt calls the "excision of motive," by which he stripped away the obvious pretexts for the characters' behavior. It is unclear what induces Iago, the villain of *Othello*, to act with such hate, or what insecurity prompts Lear, fatally, to ask his daughters to demonstrate their love for him.

His next great tragedy, *Macbeth*, was specifically written for Queen Elizabeth's successor, James I. James had become an enthusiastic patron of Shakespeare's company, now known as the King's Men. Shakespeare wrote this play involving the assassination of a king, following a failed attempt on James's life, the so-called Gunpowder Plot. At the beginning of the play, the three witches prophesy that the lineage of Banquo, James's historical ancestor, will be established on the

Scottish throne forever. If the prophesy reassured James, he would have had a more complicated response to the witches themselves. James was both fascinated and terrified by witches, whom he considered as agents of the devil. According to Greenblatt, the witches embody the principle of opacity, because their role in creating the terrible events of the play is unclear. Should one then look outward for the source of evil—to the witches—or inward, to oneself?

Chapter 12: The Triumph of the Everyday

Beginning with the composition of *King Lear*, in 1604, Shakespeare apparently had retirement on his mind. That play, in which Lear's retirement precipitates disaster, shows anxieties about the loss of status and dependency on one's children. Shakespeare seemed to have hedged against such an outcome with careful retirement planning, including substantial real-estate investments in and around Stratford. While he lived modestly in London, he would retire to a life as a country gentleman. In the last phase of his career—through which he and the King's Men continued to prosper—Shakespeare, repeatedly meditated on aging in his plays. *The Tempest*, which he probably wrote in 1611, can be considered as a summation of his career. The lead character, Prospero, has the magical power of a playwright to control and decide the fate of the other characters on his Island. In the end, he is lenient toward those who wronged him. Restored to his Dukedom, he chooses to relinquish his magic and to return home. Similarly, Shakespeare gave up scripting the fates of kings and lovers and returned to Stratford, to petty property disputes, a wife for whom he bore little love, a daughter who made an unfortunate marriage, and to a relationship he cherished, with his eldest daughter Susanna and her young family.

Media Adaptations

- *Will in the World* was released as an audio CD by Recorded Books in 2004. It is narrated by Peter J. Fernandez.

- *In Search of Shakespeare* (2004) is a four-part documentary, directed by David Wallace II and hosted by Michael Wood. The DVD is available from PBS.

- *Shakespeare in Love* is a 1998 film by John Madden, starring Joseph Fiennes as the young playwright, Gwyneth Paltrow as his love-object, and Geoffrey Rush as the theatre owner. It was written by Marc Norman and the playwright Tom Stoppard, and Stephen Greenblatt served as a consultant. The DVD is available from Miramax Home Entertainment.

Characters

Edmund Campion

Campion was a Jesuit who illegally entered England and was sojourning in the northern province of Lancashire at the same time that Shakespeare may have been there. He was the most famous Catholic martyr of the era. He beat his Protestant counterparts in a debate just before his grisly execution in 1581.

Earl of Southhampton

Henry Wriothesley, the Earl of Southhampton, was an attractive, effeminate young aristocrat. He was under pressure from his family to marry but for years he refused to do so. He was the likely addressee of many of Shakespeare's sonnets, and may have had a secret relationship with the playwright.

Queen Elizabeth I

Shakespeare lived most of his life during the reign of Elizabeth Tudor, who ruled from 1558 to 1603. Like her father Henry VIII, she was a Protestant, who reversed the policies of the brief reign of her Catholic half-sister, ("Bloody") Mary I. She supported the theater, although she was cautious about public gatherings because she feared social and political unrest.

Falstaff

Falstaff, whom Greenblatt describes as "the greatest comic character in English literature," is a character featured in the history plays *1 Henry IV, 2 Henry IV, Henry V*, and the comedy *The Merry Wives of Windsor*. Falstaff was overweight, irresponsible, and devoted to merry-making. Shakespeare modeled Falstaff after rival poet Robert Greene.

Robert Greene

The central figure in the University Wits—a group of university-educated poets and playwrights who met in pubs—the flamboyant, reckless Robert Greene insulted Shakespeare in a posthumous book, *Greene's Groatsworth of Wit*, calling him "an upstart Crow, beautified with our feathers." Greene was the inspiration for the character of Falstaff.

Hamlet

The title character of Shakespeare's most famous masterpiece, Prince Hamlet of Denmark was challenged by the ghost of his father, King Hamlet, to avenge his murder by his brother, Claudius, who married Hamlet's mother, Queen Gertrude. Hamlet is famous for his indecision about how to proceed. Greenblatt points out that his famous soliloquy, "To be, or not to be," is actually a meditation on suicide. With the character of Hamlet, Shakespeare accomplished the portrayal of a character's "inner life."

Anne Hathaway

See Anne Shakespeare

King James I

James Stuart, who was king from 1603–1625, was a more enthusiastic supporter of the theatre than his predecessor, Elizabeth. He took over the patronage of Shakespeare's company, the Lord Chamberlain's Men, renaming them the King's Men. Like Elizabeth, he feared assassination; the infamous Gunpowder Plot was a failed attempt on his life. He was the special intended audience for Shakespeare's tragedy *Macbeth*. Shakespeare used witches in its opening scene because he knew that James was both fascinated and horrified by witches.

Ben Jonson

The playwright Ben Jonson was a late contemporary and friend of Shakespeare, and a great playwright who created such satirical plays as *Volpone* and *The Alchemist*. There is a story that Shakespeare died from overdrinking at a "merry meeting" with Jonson.

King Lear

The aged title character of the tragedy *King Lear* chooses to divide his kingdom between his three daughters. His foolish request that they demonstrate their love for him sets in motion the disastrous chain of events that results in the death of his one faithful daughter, Cordelia, Lear himself, and several others. For Greenblatt, the character of Lear evokes Shakespeare's anxieties about aging.

Roderigo Lopez

The Portuguese Lopez was Queen Elizabeth's doctor. Although he was of Jewish origin, he was a professed Christian. In 1594, he was arrested on suspicion of plotting to poison Elizabeth. His conviction and execution may have inspired Shakespeare's somewhat sympathetic portrait of Shylock, the Jewish villain of his comedy *The Merchant of Venice*.

Christopher Marlowe

Marlowe was the most talented playwright in London when Shakespeare arrived on the scene in the 1580s. He was a major influence on Shakespeare and became his primary rival. Although they had similar backgrounds, Marlowe had a university degree and was part of the group of poets called the University Wits. His great plays include *Tamburlaine, Dr. Faustus*, and *The Jew of Malta*. He led a fast, daring, and dangerous life. He died in 1593, at age twenty-nine, in what was long thought to be a fight over a bill at an inn but may have been an assassination.

Prospero

The exiled Duke of Milan in Shakespeare's *The Tempest*, Prospero's magical powers make him the absolute ruler over the island where he lives with his daughter, Miranda. His control over the other characters on the island makes him like a playwright within the play. Greenblatt suggests that his relinquishing of his magic represents Shakespeare's own retirement from the theatre.

Anne Shakespeare

At age eighteen, Shakespeare married Anne, whose maiden name was Hathaway. She was twenty-six, financially independent, and about three months pregnant with their first daughter, Susanna. The legal records, including Shakespeare's will, suggests that their marriage was an unhappy one.

Hamnet Shakespeare

Shakespeare's only son died at age eleven. A variant of the name "Hamnet" was "Hamlet." The loss of his son may have been a source of inspiration for his great tragedy of that name.

John Shakespeare

Shakespeare's father, a glove maker by trade, also engaged illegally in other businesses such as wool trading and money lending. For a period, he was a prominent citizen of Stratford-upon-Avon, holding a variety of local governance positions including bailiff, the equivalent of mayor. He may have been an alcoholic, and he may also have been a secret Catholic—he possibly signed a document attesting to his private faith. During Shakespeare's adolescence, his father suffered a reversal in his fortunes—a circumstance that may have influenced Shakespeare's own drive for success and prominence.

Judith Shakespeare

Judith was Shakespeare's younger daughter and the twin of his son, Hamnet. He was unhappy with her marriage to Thomas Quiney.

Mary Shakespeare

Shakespeare's mother was born Mary Arden, a member of a prominent Catholic family with higher status than her husband John's family. She likely adhered to Catholicism despite the Protestant attempts to eliminate Catholic practice.

Susanna Shakespeare

Susanna was Shakespeare's favorite daughter. He probably retired to Stratford largely to be with her, her husband John Hall, and his granddaughter,

Elizabeth.

William Shakespeare

William Shakespeare, the Bard himself, was born in 1564 in Stratford-upon-Avon, England. In Greenblatt's account, young Shakespeare absorbed all the information and experiences that his provincial life had to offer, including the local festivals, performances by traveling players, and the pageantry of a visit to the area by the Queen in 1575. He had a grammar school education, including study in Latin, as well as a vocational education through his exposure to his father's trades in glove making and wool. He was affected by John Shakespeare's fall towards bankruptcy and by the family tensions and political dangers caused by the Protestant persecutions of Catholics. As a teenager, he may have worked as a schoolteacher for Catholic families in Lancashire. Back in Stratford, he married Anne Hathaway, though he apparently was not happy in the marriage. In the mid-1580s, he came to London, where he met John Marlowe, Robert Greene, and the rest of the group of playwrights called University Wits. Although he was influenced by their art and developed a professional rivalry with them, he was not attracted to their fast-paced, adventurous lifestyle. Shakespeare may also have had a romantic attachment to Henry Wriothesley, the Earl of Southhampton, but he was discreet about his personal relationships. He was bereaved by the death of his son, Hamnet, in 1596, and transformed the pain of this loss into the power of his tragedy, *Hamlet*. Similarly, he displayed a wondrous gift for transforming his experiences and personal relationships, as well as his imagination and source materials, into literature. He created at least thirty-seven plays, one-hundred-and-fifty-four sonnets, and two longer poems. His industriousness earned him not only everlasting artistic fame, but also the achievement of his worldly goals—the financial prosperity and social standing of a gentleman. He retired to Stratford around 1611, to New Place, the second largest house in town. He died in 1616.

Shylock

The villain of Shakespeare's *The Merchant of Venice*, Shylock was not a one-dimensional character like his counterpart, Barabas, the Jew in Marlowe's *The Jew of Malta*. He insisted on his humanity: "If you prick us do we not bleed?"

John Somerville

A distant relative of Shakespeare, John Somerville was arrested in 1583 and executed as a Catholic traitor.

Will

See William Shakespeare

Henry Wriothesley

See Earl of Southhampton

Themes

Family and Family Life

Family relationships are a major theme in Shakespeare's plays and a major theme in *Will in the World*. Especially important are marriage and fatherhood. According to Greenblatt, Shakespeare's marriage to Anne Hathaway was an unhappy one. He chose to live apart from her for most of their married life, and on dying he left her only his "second best bed." In the plays, although the comedies end in marriages and some of the tragedies involve married couples, Shakespeare expresses a sour view of the prospects for happiness in marriage. Shakespeare may have had complicated emotions about his father, John, who was prominent and prosperous during Will's early childhood but lost status and money during his young adulthood. One of the recurring themes in the plays is the "dream of restoration," in which characters are restored to their former happiness. Shakespeare's own son, Hamnet, died at age eleven, a loss that possibly inspired Shakespeare's masterpiece, *Hamlet*. Later plays, such as *King Lear* and *The Tempest* show his interest in father-daughter relationships. He had two daughters, Susannah and Judith, and he clearly favored Susannah, the first born. Greenblatt concludes that Shakespeare retired to Stratford to live with Susannah and her family.

Religion

Shakespeare's England was troubled by extreme religious conflict, with the Protestant Queen Elizabeth attempting to root out Catholicism from the land. As a youth, Shakespeare might have experienced a household that was divided by this conflict; his mother came from a prominent Catholic family, and his father, as a town official, had to enforce the anti-Catholic policies. Before he began his career as an actor and playwright, Shakespeare may have worked as a school teacher in Lancashire, a northern province that was a stronghold of recusants, or people who refused to adopt Protestantism. Greenblatt argues that the play that many consider to be Shakespeare's greatest, *Hamlet*, is shaped by this conflict. He contends that the play grew out of the anxiety created by the abolition of Catholic rituals and beliefs concerning the dead, especially the belief that the deceased were held up to suffer in purgatory before they could move on to Heaven. The Protestants pronounced Purgatory to be a falsehood. Just as Hamlet is troubled by the unsettled state of his father, who returns as a ghost, Shakespeare may have been troubled about the soul of his dead son, Hamnet, and the approaching death of his father.

Success and Social Status

In Shakespeare's youth, his father, John, was successful in a number of business enterprises and enjoyed considerable status as a local government official. However, whether because of alcoholism, religious conflict, or a combination of factors, he fell on hard times financially and lost his status. Greenblatt depicts Shakespeare as quite industrious and concerned with status. As a playwright, he worked diligently, turning out an average of two plays a year; he also had a major financial stake in his theater company. Although, unlike his rivals, the University Wits, he only had a grammar school education, he became London's leading playwright. He renewed his father's application to be officially recognized as a gentleman with a coat of arms, and he retired to the second largest house in Stratford having fulfilled his "dream of restoration."

Types of Shakespearean Plays

A number of literary genres are important to *Will in the World*. As a child, Shakespeare would have been exposed to late medieval forms, such as morality plays and mystery cycles. Morality plays were allegories performed by traveling players, in which the characters stood for abstract principles, such as Virtue or Pride, and the plays taught clear lessons. Mystery cycles were part of folk festivals and belonged to the Catholic culture that the Protestant government was trying to eliminate. They involved re-enactments of Bible stories, such as the Crucifixion. This folk culture was a clear influence on Shakespeare's adult work as a playwright.

Topics for Further Study

- How did you become you? Greenblatt introduces his study of Shakespeare's life by asking: "How did Shakespeare become Shakespeare?" This is a more complicated question than it appears to be. It is not a question of how Shakespeare became the person that he did, but rather how he came to express himself through such an amazing body of literature. Similarly, one can wonder about the influences that add up to any creative expression. How about yours? Whether you are a poet, an actor, a future doctor, or someone who prefers to keep quiet, write a two-page essay explaining how you became you, as you express yourself to the outside world.

- Write a Shakespearean Sonnet. It should be in iambic pentameter, with Shakespeare's signature rhyme scheme: a b a b c d c d e f e f g g. That is, each of the fourteen lines should have ten syllables, with the accent on the even syllables. The first and third lines rhyme; the second and fourth lines rhyme, and so on through the twelfth line. The thirteenth and fourteenth lines rhyme, forming what is called a heroic couplet. Use one of his sonnets as a model. As important as the form is the content. Greenblatt suggests that any conclusions one might draw about Shakespeare from his sonnets must be the result of inference. With this in mind, you should write your sonnet in such a way that some of the references can only be fully understood by your close friends or family.

- Watch a film version of a Shakespeare play, either a direct adaptation, such as Kenneth Branagh's 1993 *Much Ado About Nothing*, a modernization, such as *William Shakespeare's Romeo + Juliet* (1996), directed by Baz Luhrmann, or a "based on" adaptation such as Fred M. Wilcox's *Forbidden Planet* (1956), based on *The Tempest*. Write a one-page essay in which you discuss how the movie interprets the play for a modern audience.

- Greenblatt only discusses a handful of Shakespeare's plays at length. Choose one that is not listed on many pages, if at all, in the index for *Will in the World*, and write a two-page book report about some aspect of the play in relation to what you can learn about the period in which it was written.

Shakespeare excelled and innovated in the three forms of plays he worked in: histories, comedies, and tragedies. His history plays, such as the *Henry VI* trilogy that helped to establish him as a leading playwright in London, are based on chronicles of earlier times in England or on classical materials, as with *Julius Caesar* and *Anthony and Cleopatra*. These feature some of his most memorable characters, such as the evil hunchback Richard III, in the play of that name, and Falstaff, the lighthearted, irresponsible companion to young Henry V in *1 Henry IV*.

Shakespeare's comedies have conventional plots through which the lovers overcome adversity and misunderstanding in order to be joined in marriage. At the same time, Shakespeare manages to have complex explorations of theme. The comedies that Greenblatt discusses most are *The Merchant of Venice*, in which the villain, the Jew Shylock, becomes the focal point of the play, and *The Tempest*, the last play Shakespeare wrote as the sole playwright, in which the character Prospero acts as a playwright within the play, controlling the circumstances and deciding the fates of the other characters.

At perhaps the zenith of his career, Shakespeare wrote four tragedies that are among his most studied and performed works: *Hamlet, Othello, King Lear*, and *Macbeth*. Like all tragedies, these end with the downfall of the title characters. According to Greenblatt, Shakespeare's great innovation is the "excision of motive." That is, rather than making it clear why his characters behave as they do, essentially dooming themselves and others through their behavior, Shakespeare leaves out this information, making their motives into fascinating mysteries.

Like other Elizabethan playwrights, Shakespeare did not write in ordinary language but, principally, in blank verse. Blank verse is a poetic form that employs non-rhyming lines of iambic pentameter: ten syllables per line, with the accent on the even syllables. In addition to his plays, he was an accomplished poet. His poetic works include 154 sonnets. He was an innovator of the sonnet form, which consists of fourteen lines of iambic pentameter. His version, known as the

Shakespearean Sonnet, includes three quatrains, or stanzas of four lines with alternating rhymes, and ends with a rhyming couplet. His sonnets deal principally with themes of love, addressed to still unidentified persons, especially an aristocratic young man and a "dark lady." Shakespeare's longer neoclassical poems, which re-tell the classical myths of "Venus and Adonis" and the "Rape of Lucrece," were enormously popular in his day.

Style

Speculative Biography

Will in the World is a biography of William Shakespeare. Biography is a word derived from Greek, meaning life (bio) writing (graphy). Traditional biographies rely on source materials to reconstruct the life of their subject, or the person the biography is about. These can include legal records, letters, diaries, and contemporary accounts by people who knew the subject. Unfortunately, there is not enough source material to provide a detailed picture of the man who wrote such masterpieces as *A Midsummer Night's Dream* and *Hamlet*. What Greenblatt does, then, is to reach beyond the traditional bounds of the genre of biography by speculating, or making educated guesses about how Shakespeare might have lived. He combines an understanding of the historical time and place in which Shakespeare lived with the available information about Shakespeare's life and interpretations of Shakespeare's works. For example, in Chapter 1, he knows that Shakespeare was in Stratford in 1575, when Queen Elizabeth visited nearby Kenilworth; he speculates that Shakespeare might have attended the Queen's entertainments, or at least read about them, and he traces a connection between these entertainments and the play *A Midsummer Night's Dream*. Greenblatt's speculations stray from the known into the realm of the supposed, and have caused controversy and even dismissal by several critics and academics.

Elizabethan and Jacobean Ages

Shakespeare was born near the beginning of the Elizabethan Age, during which the ruler of Britain was Queen Elizabeth I (1558–1603), and he worked and lived into the Jacobean Age, under James I (1603–1625). Despite the long reigns of these monarchs, the period from the mid-sixteenth to the mid-seventeenth centuries was one of great social change within England, accompanied by political unrest. The religious conflicts that were set in motion when Henry VIII, Elizabeth's father, left the Roman Catholic Church were a constant source of fear and violence. Both Elizabeth and James were in constant fear of assassination. Greenblatt describes a time that was heavily legalistic, with constant petty lawsuits and criminal prosecutions. "London was a nonstop theater of punishments" where offenders were tortured and sometimes executed in public. Daily life was strictly regulated, but this was also a time when someone like Shakespeare could leave his hometown and his father's profession, and rise up in the world. Finally, this period was a heyday for literature and especially drama: Shakespeare was the foremost of many playwrights and poets to flourish during the Elizabethan and Jacobean Ages.

Contemporary Culture

The context for *Will in the World* is our own—a world in which William Shakespeare is very much alive as the most influential and popular literary artist in the English language, and maybe all languages. His influence goes well beyond literature: he permeates our culture. His plays *Romeo and Juliet, Julius Caesar, Hamlet*, and *Macbeth* are among the most commonly taught works in high school English. Students of those plays might recognize such lines as:

> "What's in a name? that which we call a rose / By any other name would smell as sweet" (*Romeo and Juliet* act 1, scene 2)

> "Et tu, Brute!" (*Julius Caesar* act 3, scene 1)

> "To be or not to be, that is the question" (*Hamlet* act 3, scene 1)

> "Out, damned spot! out, I say!" (*Macbeth* act 5, scene 1)

More significantly, those lines would be familiar to many people who have not read the plays. They have been absorbed into our popular culture. Similarly, Shakespeare's plays are regularly performed; many have been adapted as films, and many have been reinterpreted in modern forms. For example, the adaptations of *Romeo and Juliet* include an opera by Charles Gounod, a ballet with music by Sergei Prokofiev, the musical *West Side*

Story by Stephen Sondheim, and several films, including one directed by Baz Luhrmann with Leonardo DiCaprio and Claire Danes in the lead roles. Similarly, the comedy *The Taming of the Shrew* has been adapted as a musical, *Kiss Me Kate*, and a movie, *Ten Things I Hate About You*, set in a modern high school. Shakespeare is such a lasting and pervasive presence in our culture that it is difficult to imagine what it would be like if he had never existed.

Accordingly, there is a great deal of interest in the man as well as the works, such that a biography of Shakespeare—nearly four hundred years after his death—could well be a popular and commercial success. In his review of *Will in the World* for the *London Review of Books*, Colin Burrow complains that Greenblatt's biography is selling much more briskly than, for example, *King Lear*: "People are a lot more likely to buy books about Shakespeare's life than they are to buy books by Shakespeare." Yet it is natural to be curious about the Elizabethan man whose imagination has had such a role in shaping today's world. In his "Preface," Greenblatt himself asks, "How is an achievement of this magnitude to be explained? How did Shakespeare become Shakespeare?"

Academia

There is another relevant context to *Will in the World*: academia, or the professional world of higher education. This is the context that Greenblatt emerges from, as an English professor at Harvard University. Most academics write books and articles that are read only by other academics. A few, like the historian Simon Schama, Greenblatt's Harvard colleague Louis Menand, the literary critic Harold Bloom, and Greenblatt himself, achieve such pre-eminence within their fields that they are able to cross over and write for a general educated audience. Greenblatt has achieved so much influence and stature within academia that, even before *Will in the World*, he has become known outside of it. He is perhaps the best-known scholarly literary critic of the early twenty-first century. As Christina Nehring writes in her review of *Will in the World* for the *Atlantic Monthly*, the project represents a meeting of "the biggest literary genius of all time and the biggest literary scholar of our own time." Some scholarly readers, however, are suspicious of books like *Will in the World* that are written for non-specialized audiences. They consider them simplistic, watered-down, and insufficiently documented. It is not coincidental that some of the book's harshest critics, like Colin Burrow in the *London Review*, are also professors of English who specialize in Shakespeare.

At the same time, it may be useful for general readers to recognize the traces of more specialized writing in *Will in the World*. Instead of closely documenting his sources with footnotes, Greenblatt provides "Bibliographical Notes" for each chapter near the end of the book. At moments, such as when Greenblatt writes, "London was a nonstop theater of punishments," the reader can hear an echo of the

French social philosopher and theorist Michel Foucault. Foucault, the author of *Discipline and Punish: The Birth of the Prison*, is very influential in academia, and particularly in Greenblatt's critical method, New Historicism. Finally, near the end of the book, one finds a version of an argument that Greenblatt presented in an earlier, more scholarly book, *Hamlet in Purgatory*.

Critical Overview

One of the noteworthy aspects to the criticism of *Will in the World* is that there is so much of it. The book has drawn an enormous amount of notice for a book by a literary critic and about a literary topic. Within months of its publication, it had been featured in most book review sections of newspapers and magazines in the United States and England. Overall, this criticism has been favorable. That is, it has received far more positive reviews than negative ones. For some critics, Greenblatt has written the best of the Shakespeare biographies, surpassing his predecessors through his insightful connections between Shakespeare's life and his works. Typical of these is Adam Gopnik, who reviewed *Will in the World* for the *New Yorker*:

Greenblatt's book is startlingly good—the most complexly intelligent and sophisticated, and yet the most keenly enthusiastic, study of the life and work taken together that I have ever read. Greenblatt knows the life and period deeply, has no hobbyhorses to ride, and makes, one after another, exquisitely sensitive and persuasive connections between what the eloquent poetry says and what the fragmentary life suggests.

Other reviewers agree in praising Greenblatt's insightfulness, and they also commend his literary style as elegant and eloquent, without calling attention to itself. Yet they are less persuaded than

Gopnik by Greenblatt's articles. Colm Toibin, writing for the *New York Times*, sums up the view of several critics that Greenblatt is too willing to engage in guesswork, or to base claims on insufficient evidence: "Almost every step forward in reconstructing his life involves a step backward into conjecture and a further step sometimes into pure foolishness."

Christina Nehring, in the *Atlantic Monthly*, is less concerned with Greenblatt's conclusions than with his critical method. She deems Greenblatt's New Historicism, the practice of placing literature in its historical context to show how texts are shaped by cultural forces, to be inadequate as a way of explaining Shakespeare. The power of *Hamlet*, she argues, cannot be explained through reference to Elizabethan religious conflicts. Shakespeare's art is timeless—it evokes themes and emotions that transcend any particular historical period.

Nehring's response, however, is somewhat unusual. Most of the critics address their comments to Greenblatt's speculations about Shakespeare's life and its connection to his works. Many, like Gopnik, consider these speculations to be convincing. They praise *Will in the World* as a spectacular achievement. Others, like Toibin, are less persuaded, and their reviews are mixed or negative.

What Do I Read Next?

- Shakespeare's plays and poetry are available in many editions, both print and online. Some of the plays that Stephen Greenblatt discusses at length are *Hamlet, Henry IV Part One, King Lear, Macbeth, The Merchant of Venice, A Midsummer Night's Dream, The Tempest, The Winter's Tale*, and the sonnets.

- Stephen Greenblatt's *Hamlet in Purgatory* (2001) is a more extended discussion of the themes in "Speaking with the Dead," Chapter 10 of *Will in the World*.

- *The Greenblatt Reader* (2005), edited by Michael Paine, collects scholarly and journalistic essays by Greenblatt, the founder of the school of literary criticism known as New Historicism or cultural studies.

- In her essay *A Room of One's Own*, Virginia Woolf imagines what might have happened if Shakespeare had a sister that was as gifted as he was. Would she have become a great playwright, too? The essay is available in various editions, including one by Harvest Books, 1989.

- *Nothing Like the Sun: A Story of Shakespeare's Love-Life* (1964) is a historical fiction novel by Anthony Burgess, the author of *A Clockwork Orange*.

- In his short story "Shakespeare's Memory," the celebrated Argentine author Jorge Luis Borges imagines the consequences when an aging Shakespearean scholar inherits Shakespeare's memory. The story is available in English in his collection *The Book of Sand* (1977).

- *The Reckoning: The Murder of Christopher Marlowe* (1995), by Charles Nicholl, is a lively historical novel about the life and violent death of Shakespeare's most famous rival. Marlowe's plays, including *Tamburlaine, Dr. Faustus*, and *The Jew of Malta*, are available in many editions, both print and online.

Sources

Burrow, Colin, "Who Wouldn't Buy It?" in *London Review of Books*, www.lrb.co.uk/v27/n02/burr01_.html (January 20, 2005) Gopnik, Adam, "Will Power: Why Shakespeare Remains the Necessary Poet," in the *New Yorker*, September 13, 2004, p. 90.

Greenblatt, Stephen, *Will in the World: How Shakespeare Became Shakespeare*, W.W. Norton, 2004.

Miller, Laura, "The Genius Next Door," in *Salon.com*, www.salon.com (September 27, 2004).

Nehring, Christina "Shakespeare in Love, Or in Context," in *Atlantic Monthly*, December 2004, pp. 129-34.

Stevens, Paul, "Pretending to be Real: Stephen Greenblatt and the Legacy of Popular Existentialism," in *New Literary History* Vol. 33, Issue 3, 2002, pp. 491, 501, 505.

Toibin, Colm, "Reinventing Shakespeare," in the *New York Times*, October 3, 2004, Sec. 7, Col. 1, p. 22.

Further Reading

Bevington, David, *Shakespeare*, Blackwell, 2002.

> Bevington is a major Shakespeare scholar and editor of his plays. Shakespeare examines major themes that Shakespeare uses throughout his plays, such as love, jealously, hate, and family ties, and how these universal themes allow twenty-first century readers to enjoy and understand these plays written over four hundred years ago.

Bloom, Harold, *Shakespeare: The Invention of the Human*, Riverhead Trade, 1999.

> Bloom, one of the most renowned literary critics of contemporary times, makes the controversial assertion that Shakespeare taught humanity how to be human.

Garber, Marjorie, B., *Shakespeare After All*, Pantheon, 2004.

> Shakespeare After All is a readable and comprehensive critical study of Shakespeare's plays.

Kermode, Frank, *The Age of Shakespeare*, Modern Library, 2004.

> Kermode provides an authoritative

account of the history and culture of Elizabethan England in relation to the plays.

Schoenbaum, Samuel S., *Shakespeare's Lives*, Oxford University Press, 1991.

Shakespeare's Lives is the definitive history of the biographies of William Shakespeare.

—————————, *William Shakespeare: A Documentary Life*, Oxford University Press, 1971.

In this volume, Schoenbaum collects the primary documents related to Shakespeare's life.

Wood, Michael, *Shakespeare*, Basic Books, 2003.

Shakespeare is the companion volume to In Search of Shakespeare, a 2003 documentary hosted by Michael Wood for the BBC.